Original title:
The Magic of Christmas Candy

Author: Alec Davenport
ISBN HARDBACK: 978-9916-90-874-7
ISBN PAPERBACK: 978-9916-90-875-4

Sugary Wishes from the North Pole

Elves whip up treats, oh what a sight,
Gumdrops and fudge, a sweet delight.
Santa's belly shakes with glee,
Eating candy while sitting on a tree!

Frosting so thick, it’s like a spread,
Candy canes dance, it’s all in your head!
Hot cocoa spills, marshmallows fly,
Everyone joins in the sugary high!

Trimming Trees with Edible Cheer

Garlands of gummies strung up with flair,
Chocolate ornaments hang in the air.
Candy corns now hang from the boughs,
Watch out for the cat, she’s eyeing them now!

Cookie dough stars, and lollipop moons,
This tree's adorned with sweet little tunes.
Tinsel made of taffy, shining bright,
Hiding the sweets makes it one tasty night!

Joyful Jumbles of Taste and Tradition

A peppermint swirl, a jellybean fight,
Kids toss around treats, oh what a sight!
Chomp on a cookie, munch on a pie,
Laughs erupt as the frosting flies!

Christmas cheer drips from every hand,
Sugar plums dance like a rock 'n' band.
Brownie bites tumble off the plate,
Who needs dinner? It's all on fate!

Winter's Bounty in a Sugar Craft

Snowmen made from marzipan bliss,
Countless cookies you simply can’t miss.
Cocoa beans glide like sleighs in the night,
With every sweet bite, everything's right!

Gingerbread houses, with gumdrops galore,
Each year they crumble—kids always want more!
Frosty the Treatman is here to stay,
In a world of sweetness, we laugh and play!

Glimmering Gingerbread

In a house made of sweets, oh what a sight,
Gingerbread men dance under twinkling light.
With icing on faces and gumdrops in hand,
They giggle and wiggle, a sugar-fueled band.

The dog tries to lick, but he's met with a broom,
While the cat on the shelf eyes the candy cane plume.
Oh, gingerbread wonders, so funny and bright,
In this sweet little world, everything feels right.

Twisted Treats and Treats Untold

Licorice lollipops spin in a daze,
Marshmallow monsters dance in a haze.
Chocolate-covered dreams take a wild leap,
While jellybeans tumble in a colorful heap.

The peppermint sticks march in a row,
A brigade of sweets stealing the show.
Swedish fish swimming in hot cocoa seas,
Creating a chaos that's sure to please.

Whimsical Wrapper Wonders

Wrapped up in foil, oh what a surprise,
The sweets come alive with big googly eyes.
They jump from the bowls, causing quite a scene,
With each crinkly wrapper, they're the candy machine.

The caramel carrot hops in the air,
While truffles and taffy giggle without care.
In their colorful chaos, there's laughter and cheer,
Every unwrapped wonder brings joy near and dear.

Tinsel and Toffee

Toffee whispers secrets, oh so divine,
While tinsel-topped chocolates sip sugary wine.
Each bite brings a chuckle, a giggle, a grin,
As the laughter of treats echoes deep from within.

Fruitcake is sulking, “Not again, please!”
While gummy bears roll like they’re floating in trees.
In this twisted land of colorful glee,
The confections unite for a sweet jubilee.

Elfin Sugar Rush

Tiny hands in the jar, what a sight!
Gummy bears dancing under moonlight.
Lollipops giggle, giving sweet cheer,
Marshmallows bounce like they’re drinking beer.

Sprinkles fly as the elves start to play,
Candy canes twist in a comical way.
Chocolate rivers spill onto the floor,
Watch your step, or you'll be asking for more!

Peppermint sticks stuck all in their hair,
Elves with big grins, they just do not care.
Sugar plums do a little jig and sway,
While licorice whips chase the cookies away!

By midnight, the kitchen's a candy parade,
Leaving footprints of frosting, a sweet escapade.
With a wink and a laugh, they bolt from the door,
'Til next year, they’ll dream of that sugar score!

Colorful Cookie Crescendo

Under the tree, what do I see?
Cookies that giggle, as funny as can be.
Frosting that wiggles with jolly delight,
Baking the laughter that fills up the night.

Sprinkled from head to toe, so bright,
A gingerbread army, what a funny sight!
With icing smiles and gumdrop dreams,
They plot and they plan through the sweet, silly schemes.

Chocolate chip soldiers in a marshmallow moat,
Doughnuts in capes that are ready to float.
Even the brownies join in the fun,
Moonlight glinting on every sugary run.

So gather your friends for a cookie surprise,
Down with the crumbs, oh, what a rise!
With laughter and sweets all around the room,
Tummies will ache, but hearts will just bloom!

Savoring the Season

Gumdrops dance in a jolly parade,
Marshmallow snowflakes all lovingly laid.
Chocolate rivers flow down the street,
Fudge clouds whisper, "Come take a seat!"

Lollipops twirl in a sugary spin,
Jelly beans laugh, inviting a grin.
Caramel drizzles with whimsical flair,
While peanut brittle sprinkles everywhere!

Twinkling Candies in the Moonlight

Under the stars, a sweet treasure glows,
Licorice vines and taffy who knows?
Candied apples play hide and seek,
Giggling gumdrops, so sweetly unique!

The moon, a slice of cake on a plate,
Whipped cream clouds help us celebrate.
Lollies dance on the soft winter breeze,
While jellybeans nestle in cozy trees!

Festive Flavor Fantasies

Cotton candy clouds fluff up the sky,
Chocolate-coated dreams zooming by.
A banquet of treats, a colorful sight,
In the heart of the night, everything's right!

Peppermint sticks in a merry old fight,
Sour gummies giggle with pure delight.
Bubblegum echoes with laughter so loud,
As sprinkles shower down, blissfully proud!

Candied Memories

Fondant fairies flit through the air,
Marzipan castles built with great care.
Tasting the joy of each sweet little bite,
Making new memories that feel just right!

Bright bonbons wink from their sugary beds,
Yummy stories dance in our heads.
With every nibble, happiness grows,
In this candyland, love freely flows!

Glistening Goodies at Dusk

In the kitchen, what a sight,
Cookies dancing in the light.
Frosting rivers, sprinkles rain,
Sugar high, it's all insane!

Pies are spinning, cakes can glide,
Gummy bears seem to confide.
Candy canes do the cha-cha,
Taffy joins, saying “Ha-ha!”

Flavorful Fantasies

Chocolate mountains, oh so tall,
Lollipops that dare to roll.
Caramel rivers, sweet and thick,
Just don’t wear your best white slick!

Peppermint patty, what a tease,
Tickling taste buds with a breeze.
Fudge is plotting, oh so sly,
“Eat me first!” it dares to cry.

Wondrous Whisked Whispers

Whisks are spinning like a dream,
Whipped cream clouds, a frothy stream.
Chocolate chips in wild debate,
“Who’s the star? Just wait, just wait!”

Gumdrops giggle, sugar spritz,
Frosting laughter never quits.
Marshmallows bounce, a sticky race,
Who can frolic in this place?

Recipes for Joy

Mix a dash of silly fun,
Add some giggles, just for one.
Stir in sprinkles, a burst of cheer,
Baking laughter, oh so near!

Whisk together smiles and glee,
Pour in hugs, a secret key.
Bake it all ‘til warmth prevails,
Slice the joy, for love never fails.

Confectionery Chronicles

Once upon a time, oh what a sight,
Gummy bears danced under the moonlight.
Chocolate rivers flowed with sweet delight,
While licorice trees reached an amazing height.

Peppermint fairies flew round the treats,
Sipping hot cocoa in gumdrop seats.
Lollipops swayed to their sugary beats,
Crafting sweet giggles and candy feats.

A Symphony of Sugar

Candy canes waved in a frosty breeze,
Singing with lollipops, oh what a tease!
Chocolate truffles rolling with ease,
Caramel voices carried by sweet trees.

Jelly beans jived with such flair,
Swirling and twirling in sugary air.
The frosting played tunes without a care,
As everyone joined in with laughter to share.

Dreamy Frosting

Frosting clouds drift in a light sugar haze,
Sprinkling sparkles that glimmer and blaze.
Cupcake dreams in a buttery craze,
Whipped cream wishes that brighten our days.

Marshmallows float like fluffy white dreams,
In a world bursting with sweet, silly schemes.
Chasing gumdrops down candy streams,
Enjoying each bite as laughter beams.

Jingle Bell Treats

Jingle bells jangle on peppermint roads,
Riding in sleighs of jellybean loads.
Boys and girls dancing, shaking their codes,
Sharing their giggles like secret node modes.

Sugarplum buddies serve up the cheer,
With frosting smudged noses and candy near.
Every sweet moment brings happiness clear,
As jingle bell treats fill the atmosphere.

Chimes of Chocolate

In a land where chocolates sing,
A cocoa bell begins to ring.
Marshmallows dance in soft delight,
As fudge fairies take their flight.

Truffles giggle, swirl, and glide,
With candy canes all stacked with pride.
A sprinkle here, a drizzle there,
Laughter lingers sweet as air.

Frosting Fantasia

Whipped cream clouds in skies so bright,
Cupcake towers reach new height.
Gummy bears do somersaults,
While frosting pools in candy vaults.

A jelly bean serenade takes place,
As icing poets find their grace.
With licorice loops and peanut bliss,
You'll find it hard to resist this!

Licorice Lullabies

A licorice whip, so long and sweet,
Wraps up dreams in a chewy treat.
Candy corn whispers tales of cheer,
While peppermint swirls dance near.

Bubblegum breezes fill the air,
With toffee tunes beyond compare.
Suckers sway with joyful glee,
Spinning stories, just for thee.

The Elves' Sweet Shop

In the elves' shop, sugar runs wild,
Licorice strings make the winks mild.
Chocolate rivers flow like dreams,
And lollipop suns cast bright beams.

Giggling elves mix flavors with flair,
Sprinkling joy everywhere!
In every corner, a treat awaits,
With sugary magic that elates!

Enchanted Elixirs of Winter Glow

In a pot of bubbling cheer,
Sugary dreams draw near.
Jellybeans dance, twirl about,
Lollipops scream, there's no doubt!

Gumdrops play hide and seek,
Winks from the peppermint peak.
Chocolate rivers flowing sweet,
With every taste, can’t be beat!

Fudge fills the air, unmatched in delight,
While cinnamon giggles throughout the night.
Taffy pulls friends from far and wide,
Join in the fun; come take a ride!

Behold the wonders, a feast of glee,
Where sweets cover every tree.
So grab your spoon, and don’t be late,
For a sugar rush, it’s time to celebrate!

Frosting and Frolics in Frosty Air

Frosted cupcakes stack so high,
Frosting swirls like snowflakes fly.
Chasing sprinkles round the block,
Giggling fits with every knock!

Marshmallow snowmen, happy and round,
Dance in the kitchen; they're so profound.
Cookies giggle, soft and warm,
With each bite, they create a charm!

Frolic through syrupy streams,
While candy canes whisper sweet dreams.
Gingerbread houses, all aglow,
With icing paths where sweet winds blow!

So gather your pals, share a laugh,
In a world full of sugar, find your path.
With every chuckle, may joy define,
A frosty fairy tale, oh so divine!

Caramel Kisses Beneath the Mistletoe

Under the mistletoe, hearts do leap,
As caramel kisses make you weep.
Syrupy smiles, sticky and sweet,
With every bite, you can't be beat!

Chocolate hugs wrapped up in dreams,
Make merry giggles burst at the seams.
Fudgy laughter fills the air,
Who needs cash when sweets do share?

Naughty or nice, who can tell?
When gummy bears ring the Christmas bell.
Filling the stockings, oh what a sight,
Sugar-spun wishes take flight tonight!

So pucker up, don’t lose your cheer,
Celebrate joy while candy’s near.
With longing glances at candy jars,
Kisses bestowed beneath the stars!

A Carnival of Flavors in Winter's Embrace

Step right up for a feast of fun,
With lollies and chocolates; oh, what a run!
Flavorful laughter fills every lane,
As caramel hugs ease all the pain.

Sours and skittles in colors bright,
Whip cream storms in a joyful flight.
Come taste the season, wrapped in delight,
Where candy can make everything right!

Waffles stack higher, oh what a tease,
This snicker-doodle has so much cheese.
Every morsel, a ticket to bliss,
Tell me, who could resist such a kiss?

So embrace the cheer, let it unwind,
With flavors swirling, leave sorrows behind.
In this carnival, let joy take the lead,
Where every treat is a scrumptious creed!

Frosty Fables and Treats

In a town where snowflakes dance,
Gumdrops sparkle, take a chance.
A candy cane slipped on the ground,
Made a snowman spin around.

Marshmallow fluff in winter's breeze,
Tickling noses, oh what a tease!
Lollipop trees, bright and sweet,
Turned the sidewalks into a treat.

Chocolate sleds on peppermint roads,
Brought laughs as they shared their loads.
With every snack, a giggle grew,
Who knew sweets could be so askew?

Popcorn balls on frosty nights,
Jumping squirrels in candy fights.
Under the stars, laughter flies,
As sugar sprinkles light the skies.

Sparkling Sugar Sensations

Bubbling pots of bubbling goo,
Gummy bears in a line for two.
Marzipan pigs, they dance with glee,
Chasing licorice trees, can you see?

Jolly gumdrops with hats so tall,
Juggled by elves who trip and fall.
Cotton candy clouds in the moon's glow,
Make even Grinchy hearts overflow.

Peanut brittle on the frosty ground,
Crunchy treats that make silly sounds.
With every nibble, a joke's in store,
Sweets cause laughter, who could ask for more?

Sour balls spinning on the fly,
Tickling tongues that just can’t lie.
Laughter rings, as candy flies,
Who knew sugar held such surprise?

Cheery Candies of the Hearth

Gingerbread houses all aglow,
With icing rooftops, ready to show.
Elves sticking noses in the dough,
Wait till it bakes, what a show!

Chocolate rivers flowing wide,
Marshmallow boats go for a ride.
Willy Wonka would surely cheer,
As candies invite all near.

Fruitcake pigeons cooing in trees,
Baking blunders bring giggles and wheeze.
As frosting drips and sprinkles fly,
A sugary mess—oh my, oh my!

Taffy pulls in the wintry air,
Sing-song laughter dancing everywhere.
Share a chuckle, pass it along,
With every sweet, the joy is strong.

Sweet Secrets of the Season

Old St. Nick with jelly beans,
Wobbling down the snowy scenes.
He tripped on gumdrops off the roof,
Spinning round like a goofball woof!

Peppermint swirls with silly grins,
Sneaky elves wearing bubble chin.
Giggling candies hiding away,
In pockets for a sneaky play.

Taffy tug-of-war, the funny game,
Chewy challenges, who's to blame?
Sugary giggles fill the air,
Grabbing sweets from here to there!

Frosting fights that make a mess,
Leave us laughing, what a quest!
Under twinkling stars we sing,
For sugar-coated joy they bring.

Cocoa Dreams by Candlelight

Sipping cocoa by the glow,
Marshmallows dance and sway so slow.
Whipped cream mountains rise so high,
A droplet lands, oh my, oh my!

Ginger snaps with nutty crunch,
Who knew they could pack a punch?
Sprinkled sugar, twinkling bright,
I want to eat them all tonight!

Chocolate rivers, candy banks,
I'll build a fort with all my thanks.
A candy cane for every call,
I'll snack until I can't stand tall!

Holiday Confections

Peppermint sticks and jelly beans,
Dancing on plates like sugar queens.
Frosting fights in the kitchen space,
Why can't I cover my whole face?

Caramel pools of gooey bliss,
If I could dive, I wouldn’t miss.
Peppery nutmeg smells the air,
Sprinkled laughter everywhere!

Chocolates wink from every shelf,
I’ll sneak a few – not by myself!
Cookies stacked like tiny towers,
Let's raid the pantry for more power!

Sweetness Under the Tree

Under the tree, a sweet surprise,
Gumdrops flashing, oh what a prize!
Chocolate squirrels with crunchy tails,
Munching away, no room for fails.

Fudge so rich, a cocoa dream,
It's like a chocolate-covered theme!
Tiny elves in candy suits,
Are they guarding my gummy fruits?

Oh jelly, oh jam, let's not delay,
A sugar rush leads us astray.
Laughter and nibbles fill the air,
Feels like magic, without a care!

Nostalgic Nibbles

Taffy pulls and stretches wide,
With every chew, I laugh and slide.
Licorice ropes that test my might,
Tangled candies, oh what a sight!

Candied apples, oh how they gleam,
Taking me back, living the dream.
Cookie tin with a lid that’s stuck,
I fight it open, wish me luck!

Spritz cookies with icing stars,
Biting shapes into sweet guitars.
Each bite takes me straight to when,
I snuck the stash, and did again!

Starry Confectioner’s Night

Under the tree, the sweets do gleam,
A peppermint forest, a chocolate dream.
Gummy bears dancing, oh what a sight,
Elves juggling fudge in the shimmering light.

Sprinkles are falling like stars from above,
Each candy creation, a tale filled with love.
Marshmallows giggle as they float down the lane,
While licorice curls like a festive parade.

Taffy is stretching, it's quite the affair,
Cinnamon reindeer prance without care.
Lollipops twirl in the frosty air,
With each sugary swirl, there's laughter to share.

So gather around, let the chaos begin,
With chocolate chip laughter and smiles full of sin.
A night full of sweetness, just take a bite,
In this wondrous realm, everything feels right.

Tintinnabulation of Treats

Jingle bells echo, and candy canes sway,
Gingersnap giggles brighten the day.
Sugarplum fairies tossing sprinkles so wide,
While peppermint patties play hide and seek, side by side.

Nuts in the oven do a silly dance,
With fudge on the table, let's take a chance.
Marzipan monsters hop off the plate,
Caramel rivers make everyone late.

Chocolate-covered giggles are spilling with cheer,
Baking is chaos, it’s the best time of year.
Every confection brings chuckles and grins,
As we crunch down the laughter, let the fun begin!

So, raise up your mug filled with cocoa delight,
Let’s toast to the sweets and the festive night.
With a sprinkle of joy and a peppermint twist,
These moments of laughter are too good to miss.

Cookie Crumble Carols

Singing of cookies, oh what a sound,
The crumbs hit the floor, all scatter around.
Chocolate chip verses, a sprinkle of cheer,
With laughter and joy, the season is here.

In the oven, the treats rise with a smell,
Each one is a story, a sweet tale to tell.
Frosting and giggles mix on a plate,
The fun doesn't stop, it's never too late.

A gingerbread man with a dash of despair,
Lost his gumdrop buttons, but who would care?
With frosting on noses and smiles so bright,
We feast on the crumbles through the magical night.

So gather your friends and let's sing out loud,
In a chorus of cookies, let's be proud.
With laughter and crumbs strewn across the floor,
Each bite is a giggle, who could ask for more?

Whipped Cream Wishes

A dollop of dreams on a cup so tall,
With marshmallow clouds, we'll have a ball.
Whipped cream mountains topped with a cherry,
Sipping on joy, it's seasonally merry.

Elves in the kitchen, oh what a team,
Stirring the fun, in a frosty dream.
Cocoa rivers flow, full of whimsy and cheer,
Let's dive in the wonder, for it's that time of year.

Spray can of laughter, no silly reject,
With whipped cream mustaches, we're perfect in effect.
Everyone's giggling, sharing each treat,
Creating a party with every sweet beat.

So raise your mugs high, let your spirits soar,
To whipped cream wishes, we'll always adore.
With laughter and joy, in every little bliss,
In the land of confections, we toast with a kiss!

Candied Joys and Sparkling Eyes

In a bowl of bright delight,
Gumdrops dance in crazy flight.
Lollipops do a jig and twirl,
Fizzy treats make children whirl.

Chocolate coins like treasure found,
Peppermint sticks spin 'round and 'round.
Marshmallow snowmen stand so tall,
Who knew sweets could bring such a brawl?

Gingerbread houses stack so high,
Frosting roofs that might just fly.
With every nibble, giggles grow,
Silly faces, it’s quite the show!

Candied joy, a wild affair,
With sticky fingers everywhere.
In this party, laughter reigns,
Sweets ignite our playful veins.

A Festive Feast of Sweets

A platter stacked with treats so bright,
Sugar rush in the morning light.
Candy canes in a silly pose,
Laughter erupts with every nose.

Chocolate fountains, flowing bliss,
Dare to take a dip? Don't miss!
Puffed up marshmallows, soft and round,
In our bellies, joy is found.

Sprinkles fly like confetti cheer,
With every bite, there's nothing to fear.
Elves slip on jelly bean spills,
Delightfully messy, oh what thrills!

Sweet treats scattered, a playful mess,
We laugh and scream, "Oh, nothing less!"
Around the table, we munch and play,
Sweets on the list, hip-hip-hooray!

Tasting Tradition

Baking cookies, oh what a sight,
Flour flying, what a delight!
Rolling dough, we sing a tune,
Watch for the cat, oh what a boon!

Sprinkled tops and chocolate chips,
Savor each bite, no time for slips.
Stories told of recipes grand,
With sticky fingers, we make our stand.

Fudge so rich, we can’t resist,
One more piece? Just one, sweet bliss!
Grandma’s secret, a dash of love,
All the flavors, fit like a glove.

In this kitchen, happiness flows,
With every treat, our laughter grows.
Traditions wrapped up tight with cheer,
In every nibble, joy is near.

Holly and Honey

Underneath the sparkle bright,
Jelly beans bring pure delight.
Sticky fingers, do not fret,
Who knew sweets could bring such sweat?

Toffee crunch, a splendid sound,
Savor treats all around.
Berries covered, sweet and neat,
Giggles chase with every treat.

Peppermint snowflakes dance and play,
On this wonderfully wacky day.
Laughter rings as we all dive,
Into the feast that makes us thrive.

Holly leaves as crunch we munch,
Sweetened wishes with every lunch.
Joy abounds in every bite,
In this candy world, we feel so light.

Sweet Whispers of December

Oh, tiny treats tucked in red and green,
They sparkle and shimmer, a sugary sheen.
Gumdrops and chocolates, a curious sight,
I nibble them softly, my heart feels light.

The elves in the kitchen, so cheeky, so sly,
Sneaking all goodies as I walk by.
A bite of peppermint, a laugh and a sigh,
Who knew that sweets could make time fly?

Sticky fingers reaching for jars on the shelf,
When no one is watching, I indulge by myself.
Lollipops towering like trees in the sun,
Each sugary swirl promises endless fun.

So here's to the season, with candy to spare,
A sprinkle of laughter floats through the air.
With every sweet moment, let joy take a bow,
For December's delights are the best treats somehow.

Candy Canes and Sugar Dreams

In a world made of flavors, so wild and so bold,
I twirl with the licorice, happy and gold.
Candy canes bending, they dance in a row,
Who knew they could laugh, put on such a show?

The sugarplums giggle, they twirl in delight,
As frosting men march on this frosty night.
Chocolates are plotting a sweet little scheme,
While gummy bears giggle, lost in a dream.

Sprinkles are flying like confetti on air,
With flavors so silly that I cannot compare.
Each candy creation brings joy, oh so keen,
Making memories sweeter than I've ever seen.

So let's raise a toast to the sweets we adore,
With cheers for the gumdrops who make us want more!
In this jolly banquet of colors and tastes,
We'll gobble and savor, there's never a waste!

Frosted Delights on Winter Nights

When frosty winds blow and the snowflakes fall,
I huddle with goodies, oh what a brawl!
Marshmallows floating in cocoa so sweet,
While fudge-laden dreams dance around my feet.

A gingerbread house with a roof made of gum,
I peek through the windows, all cozy and fun.
I nibble the walls, with no hint of regret,
Each bite brings a giggle, a sugar-filled fret.

Oh, lollipop lanterns that glow in the night,
They guide all the reindeer with colors so bright.
Pretzel sticks snapping, they join in the play,
With every sweet battle, we chase woes away.

So gather your sweets, let's create and consume,
As frost paints the windows, we brighten the room.
Through frosted delights, laughter's easy to find,
In the warmth of our hearts, sweet joy is entwined.

Tinsel and Taffy: A Holiday Tale

Beneath the twinkling and shimmering glow,
I discover a stash that's hidden below.
With taffy in hand and excitement anew,
I wonder what mischief my sweet tooth might brew.

Jellybeans dancing like stars in a row,
They sway with the tinsel, putting on quite a show.
Chocolate kisses wink softly, oh my!
As I steal a few bites, I can't help but sigh.

Fudge swirls in mixing bowls, gooey and grand,
While marshmallows giggle, hand in sticky hand.
Spritz cookies tumble, a floury spree,
The sweetest of moments are waiting for me.

So join in the laughter, the flavors delight,
With candy and cheer, we'll party all night.
Through tinsel and taffy, our hearts will unite,
For this jolly adventure is just out of sight!

Merry Morsels

Sweet little nuggets, oh what a sight,
Dancing on tables, they bring pure delight.
Chocolate and caramel, a tasty affair,
Nibbling on goodies without any care.

Gumdrops are bouncing, all over the floor,
Sugarplum visions, we can't help but snore.
Sticky and messy, we laugh in a fling,
Tasting such joy, oh, the laughs that they bring.

Jolly Jellybean Journeys

A jellybean rainbow, all colors in sight,
Bouncing off walls as they take to their flight.
One gooey bite, and I break into dance,
With flavors of winter, I'm lost in a trance.

Marshmallow snowmen, they giggle and sway,
Tasting the laughter that brightens the day.
Oh, watch the parade of the jellybean crew,
Eating and giggling, there's always room for two.

Yuletide Flavors Unwrapped

Wrapped like a present, a treasure to find,
Mystery flavors all jumbled and blind.
Peppermint whispers, they tickle my nose,
A candy cane chorus in perfect repose.

Brittle and brittle, they crack and they pop,
Sour and sweet, they just never stop.
On my tongue, they twirl in a dance,
A flavor explosion, it's pure happenstance.

Tantalizing Treats of Traditions

Cookie dough giggles, all piled up high,
Chasing each other, as time speeds on by.
Gingerbread men with candy in hand,
Running through kitchens, a sweet little band.

Frosting and sprinkles, a festive delight,
They play hide and seek in the shimmering light.
With bellyaching laughter, we share all the fun,
These treats keep us smiling, long after we've spun.

Sweet Serenade Under the Mistletoe

Underneath the green-lit glow,
A candy cane's put on a show.
With each twist and every turn,
Chasing flavors, we all yearn.

Chocolate drops on frosty trees,
Laughing gnomes in winter breeze.
Wishing to be sticky sweet,
With every nibble, can't be beat.

Gumdrops bouncing, oh what fun,
Sipping cocoa, everyone!
Laughter echoes, flavors blend,
This delightful joy won't end.

Enchanted Edibles

Fudge so rich, it starts a dance,
Jelly beans in a funny trance.
Lollipops with hats so tall,
Trying hard not to drop and fall.

Marshmallow snowflakes gently swirl,
Candy corn starts to twirl and whirl.
Giggling ghosts in sugar highs,
With laughter bursting, oh what a surprise!

Silly shaped like reindeer games,
Strawberry laughter calls their names.
Dancing boldly on a plate,
Chasing dreams, we celebrate.

Sugarplum Revelations

Dreams of peppermint delight,
Dancing brightly in the night.
Gingersnap with a playful laugh,
Crafting sweets like a funny craft.

Taffy pulls and sticky trails,
Wrapped in secrets, sweetened tales.
Marzipan with a cheeky grin,
Sharing joy that comes from within.

Bonbons rolling down the floor,
Whimsical flavors begging for more.
Growing giggles in every bite,
Under twinkling stars so bright.

Candyland Adventures

A licorice lane, we stroll in glee,
Sucking on lollies by the tree.
Chocolate rivers flow with cheer,
Candy critters drawing near.

Toffee mountains, oh what heights,
Sugar squirrels in joyful flights.
Fizzy pops with flavors rare,
It's a silly, sweet affair!

Caramel roads twist and bend,
Giggling as we climb and descend.
Wrapped in sweetness, endless fun,
Candyland adventures have begun!

Delicious Dances of Delight

In a land where gummies twirl,
Lollipops spin, and marshmallows swirl.
Chocolate frolics, nuts take a leap,
While peppermint sticks giggle in heaps.

Cakes waltz on the frosty ground,
Candy canes make a zany sound.
The jellybeans slide, trip, and fall,
While taffy’s sticky, and it loves all!

Fudge flies high like a dreaming kite,
Every bite's a silly, sweetened delight.
Bonbons hop in a vibrant parade,
As jelly-filled doughnuts dash unafraid.

So join the dance, don’t sit in despair,
Chocolate rivers flow through the air.
With a twist and a twirl, let joy be your guide,
In a world where sweets and fun collide!

Hills of Honeycomb

On hills made of honey, the bees play a tune,
While gumdrop bunnies bounce under the moon.
Licorice vines swing, they twist and they twirl,
And fondant flowers bloom, oh what a whirl!

The chocolate boulders all giggle out loud,
As rainbow sprinkles gather in a colorful crowd.
A marshmallow snowman rolls down with glee,
Covered in frosting, he shouts, “Look at me!”

Candy corn critters play tag on the peaks,
With cupcake houses and syrupy creeks.
Don’t forget the lolly trees swaying with grace,
As gelatin jellies join in the race.

So come take a stroll on these hills full of cheer,
Where every sweet treat brings laughter and beer.
With each step you take, let the fun never stop,
In lands made of sugar, you’ll giggle and hop!

Chocolate Dreams in the Frost

In a world all covered with cocoa and cream,
Where fudge rivers flow and gumdrops gleam.
Toffee trees sparkle like stars in the night,
While licorice clouds bring a sugary fright.

Cadbury snowflakes tumble down from the sky,
Tickling the noses of kids passing by.
Marzipan animals prance and they play,
Making mischief in a sweet, frosty way.

Chocolate-coated icicles dangle and swing,
Life’s a delicious, whimsical fling.
With peppermint swirls spiraling about,
The cheer of the season is never in doubt.

So wrap up your dreams in frosted delight,
With every candy laugh, the future looks bright.
In a world where chocolate reigns as the king,
Join in the laughter, and let your heart sing!

Sugary Smiles Shine Bright

In a kingdom of sweet, where the lollies grin,
Every candy chuckles, full of sugary sin.
Chocolate chips wink from their crispy abode,
As candy-coated dreams fill the joyous road.

With tart little gummies that bounce and that gleam,
And cotton candy clouds, all fluffy and cream.
Brittle browsers giggle while marshmallows hum,
As jelly-filled wonders go flip-flop and thrum.

Mints dance in circles, sharp and so spry,
While cupcakes debate who's the sprightliest pie.
In this whimsical land of delightful delight,
Every sweet smile shines, oh what a sight!

So gather your friends, let the laughter ignite,
With treats all around, hearts soar like a kite.
In a world full of giggles, you'll find pure delight,
As sugary smiles keep shining so bright!

Cocoa-Kissed Wishes

In a cup so rich and round,
Hot cocoa swirls, a frothy crown.
Marshmallows bounce in a fluffy dance,
Each sip brings childlike chance.

Chocolate drips where cookies fall,
Milk mustaches, oh what a sprawl!
Santa's laugh—a hum, a grin,
With every treat, we dive right in.

Whipped cream mountains, sweet peaks high,
Sprinkles rain like a sugar sky.
With each swirl, a giggle roams,
Around the hearth, it warms our homes.

So raise a mug to the silly cheer,
Where sweetness reigns and none adhere.
For in this pot of merry bliss,
Cocoa dreams are hard to miss!

Twinkling Taffy Tales

Oh taffy pulls, a sticky maze,
Chewy wonders, a sugary craze.
Bright colors shine like a laughing rainbow,
Adventures unfold, come see the show!

Twists and tangles, a joyful fight,
Who will taste the red? What a sight!
With every stretch, a giggle may,
This playful mess is here to stay.

Twinkling tastes, a burst of fun,
Candy giggles under the sun.
Bouncing bunnies, flavors combine,
Watch them hop on candy vine!

As sweet as a kiss from a sugar beet,
In taffy tales, we find our beat.
So grab a piece, get ready to try,
For in this land, we all can fly!

Glistening Gumdrop Gardens

In gumdrop fields, sweet dreams arise,
Where jellybeans wear candy ties.
Lemon drops sparkle like sunny beams,
In this garden, reality gleams.

Bouncing gumdrops, colorful spheres,
They giggle and laugh, dispelling fears.
In every corner, a treat awaits,
In this land, joy never abates.

Marzipan hedges, sugar-coated paths,
Fickle fairies, watch for their laughs.
In flavors bold, we skip and sway,
Savoring each sweet, come what may.

So come along, don your happiest face,
In gumdrop gardens, we find our place.
With each sugary step, let laughter bloom,
In this world of sweets, we chase the gloom!

Marshmallow Mirth

A gentle cloud of fluff and cheer,
Marshmallows giggle, drawing near.
In cocoa pools, they softly float,
We’re all aboard, the sweet delight boat!

Roasting flames dance, a golden glow,
Sticky fingers, the sweetest of woe.
S'mores are calling, come join the feast,
With chocolate rivers, we’re never least!

Tiny marshmallow tales unfold,
In every hug, a treat to hold.
Puffy clouds in the chilly air,
While laughter bounces everywhere.

So toast to the fluff that brings us glee,
In marshmallow mirth, let spirits be free.
For every bite leads to a grin,
In this sweet flap, let the fun begin!

Cocoa Concoctions

In a cup of bubbly cheer,
Chocolate whispers loud and clear.
Marshmallow diving, oh what fun,
Sweetened dreams for everyone!

Stirring in a peppermint twist,
Who knew cocoa could be this brisk?
Giggling sips of fluffy foam,
It's a winter wonderland at home!

Add a dash of silly sprinkles,
Every swirl—oh, how it twinkles!
Grandpa's mustache, all chocolate smeared,
With every sip, we're all quite cheered!

Laughter echoing through the night,
As cookies vanish out of sight.
A cocoa party, oh what glee,
Mugs are empty, but hearts feel free!

Licorice Legends

A rope of black, a twisty treat,
Even gnomes would find it sweet.
Sticky fingers start the show,
“Watch me pull!” Oh, how they glow!

Legends born of chewy bends,
Like rope that never really ends.
The cat runs off with quite a prize,
A licorice tail, oh how it flies!

A game of tug, the kids take aim,
Shouting loudly, “I'm the same!”
Parents chuckle, having their fun,
As the licorice chase has begun!

Whispers of a holiday curse,
Too much candy in one big burst!
Hilarity erupts, someone fell,
In a pile, oh, what the smell!

Tasty Tidings

Gumdrops dancing, oh what glee,
Sugar-coated, wild and free.
Rainbows made of jelly beans,
Wobble wobble, fit for Queens!

Taffy pulling, sticky fun,
Stretching high, under the sun.
Grandma's secret, who would guess?
Sour surprises in a dress!

A candy cane race, oh so swift,
Half a peppermint, what a gift!
Chasing flavors, what a thrill,
Sugary laughter, time to chill!

Frosting fights and cake galore,
Sprinkling joy, we all want more!
As the kitchen’s filled with cheer,
Tasty tidings, now we're here!

Embracing Seasonal Sweets

Fudge and fudge, a ‘sugar’ cloud,
Yummy giggles, tasting loud.
Chocolate rivers flow with glee,
Marzipan boats for you and me!

Every bite, a silly dance,
Gummy bears in a goofy trance.
Do you dare to lick the bowl?
Sweets majestic, that’s the goal!

Candy canes like magic wands,
Waving joy with sticky hands.
Pudding puddles on the floor,
Winter sweetness, we want more!

Cakes and pies, let’s set the stage,
A dessert party, feel the rage!
With every treat, we can’t resist,
Embracing joy, oh, what a twist!

Cinnamon and Imagination

A sprinkle of cinnamon, oh what a sight,
The gingerbread men dance in the night,
With candy canes twirling in laughter so bright,
Marshmallows giggle, what a sweet flight!

A peppermint spiral, a goofy grin,
Chasing gumdrops, let the fun begin,
Chocolate drizzles, it's a sugary spin,
Who knew a lollipop could be so akin?

Frosting rivers flow down candy canes wide,
Unicorns bounce in a sugar-filled ride,
With licorice laughter echoing outside,
The sweetest wonders are hard to hide!

In this land of sweets, we'll never cease,
Our sugar-coated chaos, a true masterpiece,
So grab a gumdrop, let's feel the peace,
For in this flavor town, joy won't decrease!

Confectionery Cosmos

A galaxy of sweets twinkles above,
Chocolate asteroids and candy star dove,
Lollipops orbit like planets that shove,
While jelly beans giggle, oh how they love!

Marshmallow meteors streak through the skies,
With gummy worms wriggling, what a surprise,
Cotton candy clouds where dreams can arise,
In this sugary space, we're all quite wise!

Ice cream comets zooming with flair,
Sprinkling giggles and sugary air,
With licorice lighthouses shining so rare,
Nobody frowns in this candy affair!

Join the fun in this cosmic delight,
We'll dance with the chocolates, ready to bite,
In this universe of sugar, all feels right,
With sweets all around, there's pure delight!

Glittering Bites of Bliss

Jingle bells ringing with sugary cheer,
Cookies and fudge, oh let's have a beer!
With sprinkles that sparkle, we'll shout, "I'm here!"
Each glittering bite brings happiness near.

Gumdrops bouncing in a jolly parade,
While chocolate morsels perform on a stage,
With candy-coated hats, they're full of rage,
But laughter erupts, it's the sweetest wage!

Frosted delights that make smiles bloom,
As marshmallow creatures dance in the room,
Caramel rivers burst forth with a boom,
In this playful land, there's no sense of gloom!

So grab a handful of colorful fun,
Let's share these wonders, just you and me, hon,
In a world where each candy is bathed in the sun,
Together we savor, it's never outdone!

Sweet Harmony of the Holidays

Twinkling lights and treats galore,
Candy canes curl, who could want more?
Chocolate rivers flow right to your door,
In this sweet harmony, we all soar!

Marzipan swans in a graceful ballet,
Lollipops bobbing in a candy buffet,
The fruitcake nods, in a quirky way,
As sprouted gumdrops brighten the day!

With gingerbread houses, oh what a sight,
They stand all proud in the twinkling light,
While jelly beans giggle in pure delight,
In this sugary playground, all feels right!

So let's raise a toast with a fizzy cheer,
To the sweets that surround us, all gathered here,
In this sweet symphony, we sing sincere,
Wishing joy and laughter for all the year!

Confections of Joy Beneath the Tree

Under the tree, gifts stacked up high,
Sweet little packages catch my eye.
Sour gummies that dance, and minty flair,
I sneak a taste, without a care.

Candy canes lean, like they're in a fight,
The chocolate bars whisper, 'It's time to bite!'
Lollipops giggle, spinning around,
In this sugary circus, joy is found.

Fudge winks at me, silky and brown,
While jellybeans bounce, wearing a crown.
Each sweet delight causes quite the fuss,
In this candy land, we all make a mess.

Nibbles and giggles—oh what a scene!
Sticky fingers and rhythms obscene.
The tree's a treasure of flavors galore,
Who knew that sweets could lead to uproar!

Twinkling Treats for Yuletide Cheer

Twinkling lights on fluffy white snow,
Muffins that bounce and cookies that glow.
Donuts in colors, like ornaments bright,
I eat one too fast—what a funny sight!

Gumdrops in puffs, mixed with laughter,
Gingerbread houses call for disaster.
Sprinkles on toppers, oh what a thrill,
Who knew that icing could give such a chill?

Silly chocolate, oozing with charms,
Bubbling soda, exploding with psalms.
Each joyful crunch brings giggles galore,
With whirling candy spins, who could ask for more?

Peppermint whispers in frosty night air,
While swirls of licorice dance without care.
Gifts wrapped in sweet, oh what a cheer,
Our sweet holiday brings laughter near!

Chocolate Wishes in a Snowy Wonderland

In a world made of cocoa, I take a gleam,
Every chocolate whisper feels like a dream.
Marshmallows bounce in their cozy nook,
Oh, what a sight, just like a storybook!

Snowflakes of sugar cover my nose,
Brownie chunks twirl in their fuzzy clothes.
Truffles that giggle and wobble about,
With each fluffy bite, it's a frothy shout!

Minty surprises, chilly and sly,
They twiddled and twirled when I passed by.
Glee fills the air, as I savor each taste,
In this snowy delight, there's no time to waste!

Laughter erupts like boiling fondue,
With sweet little messes that spark joy anew.
Each chocolate morsel makes me rejoice,
In this flurry of sweet treats, I lift my voice!

A Symphony of Sweets at Dusk

As the sun sets low, the treats come alive,
A symphony plays, sugar vibes thrive.
Caramel threads dance and sing a tune,
While cupcakes dream under the moon.

Licorice laughs in a licorice line,
While fudge frolics, feeling so fine.
Each chewy bite brings a chuckle out loud,
In our candy orchestra, we're all feeling proud!

Tootsie rolls sway, with a sugar praised cheer,
Gumballs bounce high, filling the air with cheer.
The clock strikes the hour, and we all take flight,
In this confections' opera, we're dancing all night!

So grab a sweet, let the fun never cease,
With each bite of joy, there's instant release.
As the dusk deepens, our laughter soars,
In this sugary concert, we rejoice forevermore!

Merry Morsels for the Heart

Tiny treats, oh what a sight,
Sugar sprites dance in delight.
Chocolate drops and jelly rings,
Laughter flies on candy wings.

Fudge so rich, it makes you grin,
Sticky fingers, let the fun begin!
Gummy worms that wiggle and squirm,
Sweet madness, watch your heart warm!

Peppermint sticks with stripes so bold,
Stories of sweetness waiting to be told.
Caramel pools in a sticky mess,
Joy unfolds in this candy quest!

Lollipops that twirl like a dancer's shoe,
Happiness wrapped just for you.
In every wrapper, a giggle, a spark,
Candies brighten the cold and dark.

A Carousel of Confections and Light

Round and round, the sweets parade,
Candy canes that shimmer and fade.
Cupcakes topped with frosting skies,
Each bite a treat, a sweet surprise!

Marshmallow clouds that float up high,
Chocolate rivers that never run dry.
Sprinkles raining down like confetti balloons,
In this land of sugar, we dance to tunes!

Licorice twists that bend and sway,
A carousel turning in a candy bouquet.
Fruity delights all glimmering bright,
Spinning around in joyous flight!

Nutty brittle, crunchy and crisp,
Cocoa dreams in every luscious whisp.
Delightfully silly, this grand affair,
A carnival of flavors fills the air!

Whimsical Wonders in Every Wrapped Bite

Unwrap the giggles, what do you see?
A world of wonders, just for me!
Meringue kisses take flight like a dream,
Deliciously strange, or so it would seem!

Candy apples smile with their shiny glaze,
Like little suns on frostier days.
Chocolate-covered everything in sight,
Each nibble brings such pure delight!

Bubbles of gum that pop and fizz,
Tickle your tongue, oh yes, it is!
Bonbons wrapped like treasures so bright,
All bursting forth with sugary might!

Candy confetti, sprinkle the fun,
A party of flavors has just begun.
Laugh loudly now, let your sweet tooth run,
In this land of treats, we all are one!

Jingle Bell Jellies and Gummy Joy

Wobbling jellies in colors so bright,
Bouncing around, what a silly sight!
Gummy bears dance in sugary cheer,
Each twist and turn brings laughter near.

Licorice ropes that stretch and twine,
Right from the shelf, they hope to be mine!
Every bite’s a reason to shout,
Even grandpa can’t help but pout!

Jingle bells ring with minty kicks,
Sour blasts turn sweet with tricks.
Yummy treasures filled with fun,
Christmas treats for everyone!

So grab a handful, don't be shy,
Candy's awaits, oh me, oh my!
With every nibble, games to deploy,
What a riot, oh what joy!

Sweet Surprises Wrapped with Love

In stockings hung with cheerful glee,
A lollipop, just for me!
Chocolate coins, oh what a thrill,
They vanish fast, I mustn't spill!

Gumdrops dance on sugar peaks,
Silly smiles, the joy it speaks.
Marshmallow snowmen, plump and round,
In a candy kingdom, fun is found!

Candy canes that twist and twirl,
Each bite makes the taste buds whirl.
Brightly wrapped in colored gleam,
It's a sweet and sugary dream!

Wrapped in laughter, joy to share,
These treats bring folks together, I swear!
Sugar highs and silly chats,
All aboard the candy hats!

Holiday Hues on a Candy Canvas

This festive season, colors bright,
A canvas made of pure delight.
Glistening reds and greens abound,
In each sweet treat, joy is found!

Lollies swirl with colors bold,
These bites of joy never get old.
Fruits and flavors, mixed with cheer,
I can't resist, oh look, a deer!

Licorice ropes like winding streets,
Every corner a sugary treat.
Painted peeps in joyful rows,
Who knew sweets could come in bows?

Oh, taste the joy in every hue,
These candies share a laugh or two.
Unwrap the fun, don’t be late,
Join the feast, celebrate!

Fables of Fudge and Festive Spirits

Tales of fudge delight each tongue,
With every story, oh how it’s sung!
Minty whispers in the night,
One nibble makes the world feel right!

Gingerbread men, they start to dance,
As sugar sprinkles weave their chance.
Choco tales of winter's call,
Cuddle up, it’s fun for all!

Caramel rivers flowing sweet,
Where gummy bears find trick-or-treat.
Beneath the mistletoe they hide,
Jump for joy, oh what a ride!

So gather 'round this festive tale,
With sugary themes that never pale.
The joy of sweets is always near,
In every smile, in every cheer!

Cinnamon Stars on a Moonlit Path

Stars of cinnamon glow so bright,
On a moonlit path, what a sight!
Baking giggles fill the air,
As cookie dreams begin to stare!

Sprinkled sparkles twinkle free,
On gingerbread houses, oh, what glee!
Marzipan critters dance around,
Making mischief, silly sound!

Oh, the frosting, thick and sweet,
Decorates each happy treat.
With joyous crumbs that flutter down,
A sugar party wears a crown!

So grab a star, let laughter ring,
In this sweet chaos, joy takes wing.
The path is lined with pure delight,
Let's feast on dreams beneath the night!

Peppermint Whispers

In a jar sat a minty treat,
With stripes so bright and neat.
One took a nibble, then a bite,
Squeezed out a squeal of pure delight!

The cat pounced in, oh what a sight,
To chase the candies, what a fright!
They danced around the silver tree,
Whispering secrets, full of glee.

Sugar plums joined in the fun,
Twirling, spinning, one by one.
With laughter echoing through the room,
Sweet scents chased away the gloom!

They played hide and seek with glee,
Throwing sprinkles - oh, what a spree!
Each candy got their moment to shine,
In this crazy, festive candy line!

Frosted Delights

A gumdrop village, what a sight,
Frosted roofs, a sheer delight!
Chocolate paths that wind and twist,
A frosty wonderland, you can't resist!

Marshmallow snowflakes drift and glide,
As jellybeans jump to the side.
Fudge rivers flow, so rich and brown,
A gumdrop reign as the king of the town!

Each little treat has its own dance,
With sugar sprinkles, they twirl and prance.
Licorice sticks fencing through the night,
While toffee rocks create a sweet fight!

In this land, there's laughter galore,
With peppermint pebbles for a colorful floor.
Giggles and chuckles fill the air,
As candy critters frolic without a care!

Sweets of Yuletide Joy

A licorice tree holds candy bells,
With jellybean gifts that tell sweet tales.
Gumdrops giggle as kiddos squeal,
Under the glow of peppermints, we feel!

Hot cocoa rivers with marshmallow boats,
Sailing past chocolate cannons, whoa floats!
Whipped cream clouds drift by with cheer,
As candy canes whisper, "Joy is here!"

Sugar rushes cause the kids to zoom,
Through a forest of taffy that’s in full bloom.
With frosty concoctions shaken and stirred,
Every laugh and cheer is carefully heard!

Sprinkle a bit of silliness around,
In this sweet wonderland where joys abound.
Every color twinkles, every smile glows,
With sweets of joy, our gladness grows!

Candy Canes and Cheer

Candy canes stand in rows like soldiers,
Guarding giggles of sweet, bold holders.
With a twist and a turn, they wave hello,
In a whirlwind of laughter, they steal the show!

Ketchup-flavored? No one dares,
But licorice bridges meet comical stares!
Gingerbread houses, oh what a view,
With frosting roofs and walls made of chew!

The fruitcake jokes always take a hit,
As gumball fountains bubble with wit.
Marshmallow snowmen tumble and roll,
Bringing joy that fills the whole soul!

So grab a treat and join the fun,
Candy canes cheer, “Let’s all run!”
Under the holiday lights that gleam,
Sweet memories made, like a sugary dream!

Peppermint Wishes and Licorice Hopes

In a world where sweets collide,
Peppermint sticks take a wild ride.
Licorice ropes twist and twine,
Hoping they'll give a sparkly sign.

Chocolate dips and gumdrop trails,
Candy canes that giggle and wail.
Jelly beans bounce with a snicker,
While every tickle makes them quicker!

Marshmallow pals in a fluffy freeze,
Popping like popcorn, if you please!
With every bite, laughter flows,
Sassy sweetness, as joy overflows.

Sprinkled treats with a pinch of cheer,
As we nibble, we hold near.
To those moments wrapped in delight,
Candy giggles fill the night!

Sugarplum Serenade Under Starlit Skies

Sugarplums dance on the moonlit ground,
Wiggling and jiggling without a sound.
Marshmallow clouds fluff up the air,
As lollipop owls perch without a care.

Under starlit skies, they twirl and prance,
Jelly baby critters join the dance.
With a sprinkle of sugar, they glimmer bright,
And tickle our fancies late into the night.

With chocolate whispers drifting by,
Gumdrops giggling, oh my oh my!
A candy cane conductor leads the way,
As giddy giants jingle and sway.

Lemon drops slide down from the trees,
Wishing for wishes as light as a breeze.
In this sweet serenade, we're forever stuck,
Laughing and sharing our candy luck!

Glistening Goodies in Gingerbread Dreams

In gingerbread houses with crusty roofs,
Glistening goodies unveil their truths.
Frosting rivers swirl and flow,
While jellybean fish swim to and fro.

Ginger folk doing the sugar dance,
With chocolate drizzle, they take a chance.
Candy corn critters hop in glee,
Making wishes for their candy spree.

Fudge bunnies in a marshmallow stew,
Creating pranks, oh what a view!
Licorice vines that tangle and twist,
While cocoa whispers, “You must exist!”

Sprinkled joy cups raise a cheer,
As candy-flavored laughter draws near.
In this realm of frosting and cream,
Every moment’s a sugarplum dream!

Crystalline Confections and Cozy Nights

Crystalline confections sparkling bright,
Filling our hearts with pure delight.
Caramels giggle, all soft and sweet,
Sharing secrets in every treat.

The nighttime sky, a sugary show,
Chocolate fountains make spirits glow.
With every nibble, a chuckle rings,
Gummy bears dance with candy flings.

Cozy nights with peppermint stars,
Taffy tales travel near and far.
We sip warm cocoa, a marshmallow tide,
While caramel whispers, "Come for a ride!"

So let's cuddle up and taste the cheer,
In this world of goodies, we hold dear.
With confectionery dreams wrapped tight,
We celebrate through this sweet delight!

A Kaleidoscope of Candies and Cuddles

In a jar of colors bright,
Sugar smiles gleam in the light.
Gummy bears do a silly dance,
Chocolate coins hope for a chance.

Peppermint sticks in a row,
Whisper sweet secrets, you know.
Marshmallow fluff, a cloud so wonky,
Spreads sticky joy, oh so funky!

Lollipops spin like a top,
While jelly beans refuse to stop.
Candy canes bend with a grin,
Join in the fun, let's begin!

Tickle your taste buds, don't resist,
Each sugary bite, a dreamy twist.
With every sweet, laughter ensues,
Cuddles and giggles, the festive muse.

Sweet Memories in Every Crinkle

Rustling wrappers bring back cheer,
Toffee whispers, “Come over here!”
Every crinkle hides a delight,
A treasure discovered at night.

Caramels cling with gentle glee,
While chocolate nibbles tease with spree.
Nothing but taffy pulling a prank,
Sticking to teeth like a merry bank!

Licorice twists in a knotty race,
Making faces, it’s a silly chase.
Sour drops giggle with every bite,
Sending us off in pure delight.

Sweet scents float through the air,
A carnival of flavors everywhere.
Collecting crumbs with twinkling eyes,
In every crinkle, surprise never lies!

Sweetscape of a Winter Wonderland.

In a cottage of cookies, oh what a sight,
Gumdrops sparkles under the moonlight.
Snowmen crafted of frosted treats,
Stand guard while the candy canes greet!

Fudge flows like rivers, creamy and sweet,
While marshmallows march on their fluffy feet.
Candy flurries dance in the sky,
Lemon drops twirl and fly by!

Gingerbread houses guarded by glee,
With icing rooftops as sweet as can be.
Chocolate buttons pave the way,
To this sweetscape where giggles play.

Every heart feels light and gay,
In this whimsical world where we stay.
Taste-bud magic, come take a stand,
In this joyful, sugar-coated land!

Sugarplum Dreams

In the land of sugarplum fun,
Lollipop fairies all on the run.
Waving wands made of candy canes,
Sparking silliness in sweet refrains.

Marshmallow pillows, pillows so fluffy,
Giggling friends who get oh-so-tough-y.
Every dream drizzled with caramel beams,
Turning the night into sugary themes.

Frolicking fudge fairies with joy,
Creating silly spells, oh boy!
Chocolate rivers flow bright and bold,
In this dreamland where sweets unfold.

As the sun rises, with smiles so gleam,
In the world where everything's a dream.
Sugarplum whimsy, a whimsical dance,
Inviting us all for a sugar-filled chance!

Milton Keynes UK
Ingram Content Group UK Ltd.
UKHW020044271124
451585UK00012B/1039